F L O R E S   S E A

Komodo Island

National Park
Visitors Center

Komodo ●

+ Mt Komodo

Padar Island

Rinca Island

+ Dragon Mountain

Flores

Komodo National Park

Kraken-ka
The Komodo Dragon
A Tale of Indonesia

Written by
Jodi Parry Belknap and Tamara Montgomery

Illustrated by
Joseph D. Dodd

Joseph D. Dodd
2008

Calabash Books®
Honolulu

Endpaper Cartography: Buzz Belknap
Cultural Consultant: Dr. Kirstin Pauka, Professor of Southeast Asian Theatre,
University of Hawaiʻi at Mānoa. Thank you to Dr. Pauka for reviewing the
manuscript for cultural accuracy and for suggesting that Kraken become Kraken-ka.
Developmental Consultants: Rita Ariyoshi, Mary Bell, Carol Catanzariti, Mary Clark,
April Coloretti, Clemence McClaren; Kathryn Parry, Meredith Parry.
Educational Consultant: Amy Lin Miner, M.F.A. We greatly appreciate the expertise
of Amy Lin Miner, who brought her experience teaching secondary English and
drama and her innovative thinking to compilation of the Educational Resources and
Activities for Grades 3-5 on the accompanying CD.
Special thanks to: David Minkoff, M.F.A, Assistant Professor of Scenic Design at
the College of Santa Fe, New Mexico, whose enthusiastic assistance and considerable
computer skills were invaluable to the illustrator in preparing the colorized
version of images for the book.
We also wish to acknowledge the support of Cliff Montgomery and Buzz Belknap.

Calabash Books LLC

P. O. Box 22387
Honolulu, Hawaii 96823
email: belknappublishing@mac.com
www.calabashbooks.com

Printed in China

Once, a very long time ago, on a small island east of Bali, in the middle of the Flores Sea, a dragon was born. His name was Kraken-ka.

Naga, the Goddess of Wisdom and Beauty, created Kraken-ka. He was the first dragon on earth. When Naga saw her handiwork, she allowed herself a rare moment of pride because he was so beautiful.

Kraken-ka hatched from an egg in a sandy hole on the edge of a rain forest. His skin was deep red and dusted all over with blue, orange and yellow triangles, crescents, spirals and stripes. Big orange curves decorated with red, blue and yellow shapes rose from his back.

In the sun-dappled treetops where Kraken-ka first lived, shimmering prisms of light danced from a mosaic of turquoise on his forehead. It was as blue as the sky.

Naga gave Kraken-ka and all the other animals she put on the island one law to live by. It was:

"Take from the earth only what you need!"

Right away Kraken-ka knew what he liked to do best. Eat. It soon became his favorite thing to do. In the trees he ate beetles and grasshoppers and caterpillars and geckos and bird eggs. When he got bigger he climbed down to the ground and ate rats and snakes and deer and goats.

**"Crunch. Crunch. Crunch.
Munch. Munch. Munch."**

Kraken-ka ate and Kraken-ka grew. Big. Very big. His tail grew long, his head grew broad, his jaws grew strong and the curves on his back grew tall. Above the turquoise mosaic on his forehead, an imposing crown appeared.

When Kraken-ka ran, his tail swept back and forth and his shoulders swung from side to side. Points of light flashed from the surfaces of his splendid crown.

Kraken-ka had a special kind of tongue that worked like a nose. It was long and thin with two prongs shaped like a V. He used his tongue-like-a-nose to taste the air and catch the scent of food.

When Kraken-ka was hungry, which was most of the time, he drooled. Kraken-ka didn't know it, but his drool was poisonous.

Kraken-ka soon discovered what he liked to eat most. Spoiled meat. Sometimes he would let a water buffalo or other big animal get away after taking only one bite of it. Later, the animal would die from the poison in Kraken-ka's drool. Then Kraken-ka would use his tongue-like-a-nose to find the carcass. He especially liked decaying deer and smelly, three-day-old boar.

Before long no animal felt safe on the island. Slinky snakes, poison puffer fish, fat frogs, hairy boars, dainty deer, grizzled goats, slippery sea turtles, long-tailed monkeys, plump birds, little wild horses with bony legs, and even big, you-can't-possibly-swallow-me water buffalo with sharp pointed horns, knew what it meant when they heard the cracking of Kraken-ka's mighty jaws.

The animals learned to hide from Kraken-ka. They hid in tangled mangrove roots, on rock piles, in clumps of lemon grass, behind the trunks of coconut palms, in the branches of paperbark trees, in the lowlands and in the uplands. But Kraken-ka always found someone to eat. Or bite.

"Crack. Crack. Crack!
Crunch. Crunch. Crunch.
Munch. Munch. Munch."

Every afternoon Kraken-ka went to his favorite blue pool to take a long drink. Then he lay down in a sandy nest nearby to take a nap.

He was drinking one day when he heard a voice ask an impertinent question.

"Sssss! Do you plan to drink all that water by yourself?"

A large silver-colored Cobra snake was hanging from a Lontar palm beside the pool.

"What's it to you?" Kraken-ka said. "This is my pool."

"It's a warm day and I'm thirsty," said the Cobra, as she slithered down the palm tree and slid between Kraken-ka's legs toward the pool.

"Crack, Crack, Crack!"

Kraken-ka snapped his jaws at the Cobra, but he didn't try to bite her.

"Sssss! I wouldn't do that again, if I were you," said the Cobra, dipping her head into the water to drink. She took several sips. Then she dove into the pool and out of sight. Kraken-ka started after her but stopped when he saw his reflection in the water mirror created by the pool. It delighted him.

"Oh! What glorious colors! What perfect patterns! What an amazing shape! And look at my magnificent crown! Oh, I am so beautiful I can do whatever I want, go wherever I want, and eat whomever I like!"

Kraken-ka was so pleased with how beautiful he was that he forgot all about the Cobra. He lay down to take his nap.

The Goddess Naga lives in palaces she keeps in pools throughout Indonesia. She was at one of her favorite palaces on the day Kraken-ka met the Cobra. It was inside Kraken-ka's pool.

Naga was reclining comfortably on a lounge made of cushy lotus leaves when her rest was interrupted by the arrival of her personal emissary, the silver-colored Cobra.

"Ahem."

"Aha, my dear Cobra, welcome."

"Sssss, excuse me, O-Most-Wise and Beautiful Goddess, but I have news."

"Oh? And that is?"

"A great number of the animals…ssss on this island are disappearing."

Naga locked her gaze onto the Cobra's dark eyes.

"Disappearing? Is that so?" she asked, in a stern voice.

"It is…ssss! And they are all afraid. Except me, of course."

"And who is responsible for this dreadful state of affairs?"

"The carnage is being wrought by one of your most remarkable creations…ssss."

The Cobra waved her head toward the top of the pool. Naga looked up through it and saw Kraken-ka asleep in his nest. Pieces of leftover meat, half-chewed bones and clumps of undigested skin and hair littered the ground around him.

It was not a pretty sight.

Naga gasped. "This will not do!" she declared, and rose from her lounge in a fury.

Kraken-ka was dreaming about catching the silver-colored Cobra when he was rudely awakened by the sound of a loud gong.

Clang!

A tall being with a blue body rose from the pool. Strands of shiny white beads swung from her neck. Golden rings glittered on her fingers. A bracelet with sparkling emeralds for eyes gleamed on her wrist. The Cobra was dangling from her shoulders.

It was Naga, the Goddess of Wisdom and Beauty. She pointed a long blue finger at one side of Kraken-ka.

"A most disgusting mess!" she said. "And what is that ugly bump on your side?"

"Ugly? " Kraken-ka was shocked. He looked at his side. A big bump was sticking out from it.

"Oh, that's just a baby deer hoof, left over from my morning snack," he said. "Or maybe it's part of a Maleo bird beak, from my first meal today. Nothing to worry about."

Naga did not agree.

"How revolting! You've eaten so much and made such a mess that your colors are dusty, your patterns are crooked and your shape has changed.

Not acceptable! Not acceptable at all!"

Kraken-ka couldn't believe what he was hearing.

"Not acceptable? Not acceptable? Who are you to say that to me?"

And he opened his jaws wide and lunged at the apparition before him.

"Crack. Crack. Crack!"

Naga floated away from Kraken-ka's jaws before he could get close enough to bite her.

"Who am I? Who am I?" she cried, in a voice that boomed across the island and out into the surrounding sea.

"I am Naga, Goddess of Wisdom and Beauty! I created you!"

And with a flourish of shining jewelry, curly hair and silver-colored Cobra, she swooped down until she was nose-to-nose with Kraken-ka.

"Take from the earth only what you need!

That is the Law, and you have disobeyed it, Kraken-ka!"

Kraken-ka was too amazed to protest. He kept his jaws shut, but two big strings of drool puddled on the ground beneath them.

Naga glared at Kraken-ka. He was still one of the most beautiful creatures she had ever made.

"Kraken-ka, you have three chances to prove you can obey the Law, or suffer the consequences!"

"Three chances!"

And in a flash, Naga dropped back into the pool.

The next day Kraken-ka was too busy eating to think about Naga's warning. That night he dreamed about all the animals he had eaten or tried to eat during the day: two fresh puffer fish in the shallows of the sea, the rotting carcass of a sea turtle, an army of marsh frogs, a skinny goat he found on an open plain and a pig that got away after only one bite.

Later he dreamed that he looked into the water mirror and didn't recognize himself. The glorious colors on his back and sides were gone and his body was gray, except for a few tinges of blue.

In the morning the sound of a familiar voice woke Kraken-Ka.

"Sssss. Take from the earth only what you need, or suffer the cons...sssequences...sss!"

It was the silver-colored Cobra.

Kraken-ka was wide awake when he went to the water mirror and saw that what he had dreamed was true. His glorious red, blue, orange and yellow colors were gone. His body was gray. Only a few tinges of blue remained.

"Only two chances...ssss left!" said the Cobra, and slipped into the pool.

But Kraken-ka didn't care about his glorious colors. He didn't care about the two chances he had left, and he didn't care about Naga's warning or the Law. He was too hungry.

Later that day his tongue-like-a-nose caught a wonderful scent. He followed it to a dead water buffalo trapped in a tangle of mangrove roots. The carcass was just ripe enough to be delicious.

Kraken-ka spent the whole day eating, until his belly bulged. It was night when he finally reached the pool. The evening stars were out but it was too dark to look into the water mirror to see if anything else had changed. "Maybe I didn't need the whole water buffalo," he thought, as he settled down for his nap, "but I had to have those four chunky hooves, that tasty tail and those scrumptious ears. Yummmm. Besides, I can eat whatever I want, even if it is bigger than me."

Deep in the night a pale yellow moon rose. It shown on Kraken-ka sleeping and animals on the island leaving. The animals who stayed took advantage of the moonlight to forage for food, build their nests and hunt in peace. There were not so many of them as before.

The next morning Kraken-ka's belly still was so big it dragged on the ground.

"I'll be good as new after a cool drink," he thought, and waddled over to the pool.

Naga was floating above the water.

"I've been waiting for you. Don't be surprised at what you see."

Kraken-ka looked in the water mirror. His perfect patterns were gone. He couldn't tell triangles from crescents or spirals from stripes.

"Where are my perfect patterns? What happened to them?"

"Your perfect patterns are gone, Kraken-ka. Take from the earth
only what you need. Or suffer the consequences. That is the Law."
"Only one chance left!"

Kraken-ka spent the rest of the morning wandering in the uplands. He didn't find anything to eat. By afternoon he was very hungry again, so he headed for his special fishing place, a large tide pool in the lowlands. "A big water snake or a couple of juicy frog fish would taste good," he thought.

But when Kraken-ka reached the beach, two animals he had never seen before were sitting beside his tide pool. Patches of red and white hung on their bodies. Clumps of what looked like brown seaweed dangled from their heads. One of them was holding a grouper fish.

Kraken-ka's stomach rumbled. "I am so hungry," he thought, "I wonder what those animals would taste like."

He looked around to see if Naga was watching, but she was nowhere in sight. Just in case, he hid between a big sand dune and a jujube tree to think about what to do next.

The longer Kraken-ka watched, the hungrier he got. His tail swung back and forth. Drool dripped from his jaws. He forgot about Naga. He forgot about the Law. He forgot about his one last chance.

At last, Kraken-ka couldn't help himself. He came out from his hiding place between the sand dune and the jujube tree and went after his next meal. He opened his jaws wide and ran faster than the fastest snake in a calm sea toward the animals beside his tide pool.

The sound of a gong louder than ten thousand gamelans filled the sky.

Bong!

The earth shook. A great wave rose in the sea.

A terrifying figure descended from a cloud above the jujube tree. Curly hair flying, blue skin glowing, beads and bracelets clattering, silver-colored Cobra hissing, it was Naga, Goddess of Wisdom and Beauty, in her most vengeful form. She blocked Kraken-ka's path.

"Demon!" she cried.

For the first time in his life Kraken-ka was afraid. He dug his toes into the sand and slid to a halt. Raising his powerful tail, he ran across the beach away from Naga. He cracked his jaws together loudly.

"Crack. Crack. Crack!"

At the same moment he heard another *"Crack. Crack. Crack!"* Over his shoulder he saw something chasing him. Naga had sent an ugly black creature after him!

Kraken-ka ran. The creature ran, too. Its belly dragged on the ground. Its broad tail swung back and forth.

Kraken-ka ran faster. The creature ran faster. On each side of its jaws strings of drool whipped in the wind.

Kraken-ka stopped running and turned to face the ugly black creature. But when he did, it was gone.

Instead, Naga hovered above the sandy beach.

"You have used your three chances, Kraken-ka," she said. "Now you must accept the consequences. Your glorious colors, your perfect patterns and your amazing shapes are gone."

"My glorious colors, my perfect patterns, my amazing shapes? All gone?"

"Yes. They are all gone. And that ugly creature chasing you was only a shadow. Your shadow."

"But what about my crown? That creature had no crown."

"Your crown, too. It's gone."

Then Kraken-ka understood. He had lost his glorious colors, his perfect patterns and his amazing shapes.

He looked at Naga. "I… I am no longer beautiful, but… but… I am still hungry!"

The Goddess of Wisdom and Beauty looked at the hungry creature standing before her with strings of drool falling from its jaws. She thought, "I gave him gifts—a tongue-that-works-like-a-nose, that poisonous bite and drool, those glorious colors, perfect patterns, amazing shapes and even a crown. ...but I made him hungry, too."

Naga floated close to Kraken-ka.

Once more she said, "Take from the earth only what you need. That is the Law. You disobeyed the Law, Kraken-ka, and you have suffered the consequences."

Then Naga sighed, and because she was merciful, said, "Kraken-ka, come with me to look into the water mirror once more. You will see that I have left you a reminder that you once were the most beautiful creature on the island."

Kraken-ka followed Naga to the blue pool. He looked into the water mirror. There, in the middle of his forehead, beneath the memory of a beautiful crown that only he could see, was the shimmering mosaic of turquoise. In the right light it was still almost as blue as the sky.

Akhir

Pacific Rim

Russia

Alaska

Canada

N. Korea

S. Korea

Japan

China

United
States

Mexico

Taiwan

Hawaii

Northern
Mariana
Islands

Thailand

Vietnam

Philippines

· Guam

Marshall
Islands

Cambodia

Brunei

· Palau

Micronesia

· Palmyra

Malaysia

· Kiribati (Christmas Island)

Singapore

· Nauru

Indonesia

Papua
New Guinea

Tuvalu

East Timor

Solomon
Islands

Komodo
Island

Samoa

Vanuatu

Fiji

· Tahiti

New
Caledonia

· Tonga

Australia

New Zealand

A N T A R C T I C A